HOW TO SURVIVE A
FIRE

KENNY ABDO

Bolt!
An Imprint of Abdo Zoom
abdopublishing.com

abdopublishing.com

Published by Abdo Zoom, a division of ABDO, P.O. Box 398166, Minneapolis,
Minnesota 55439. Copyright © 2019 by Abdo Consulting Group, Inc. International
copyrights reserved in all countries. No part of this book may be reproduced in any
form without written permission from the publisher. Bolt!™ is a trademark and logo
of Abdo Zoom.

Printed in the United States of America, North Mankato, Minnesota.
052018
092018

**THIS BOOK CONTAINS
RECYCLED MATERIALS**

Photo Credits: AP Images, Alamy, Getty Images, iStock, Shutterstock
Production Contributors: Kenny Abdo, Jennie Forsberg, Grace Hansen
Design Contributors: Dorothy Toth, Neil Klinepier

Library of Congress Control Number: 2017960643

Publisher's Cataloging-in-Publication Data

Names: Abdo, Kenny, author.
Title: How to survive a fire / by Kenny Abdo.
Description: Minneapolis, Minnesota : Abdo Zoom, 2019. | Series: How to survive |
    Includes online resources and index.
Identifiers: ISBN 9781532123245 (lib.bdg.) | ISBN 9781532124228 (ebook) |
    ISBN 9781532124716 (Read-to-me ebook)
Subjects: LCSH: Survival--Juvenile literature. | Fire--Juvenile literature. |
    Emergencies--Planning--Juvenile literature. | Natural disasters--
    Juvenile literature.
Classification: DDC 613.69--dc23

TABLE OF CONTENTS

FIRE

Fire is used for many everyday needs. It is used to cook food, make light, and keep rooms warm. An **uncontrolled** fire can destroy just about anything it comes into contact with.

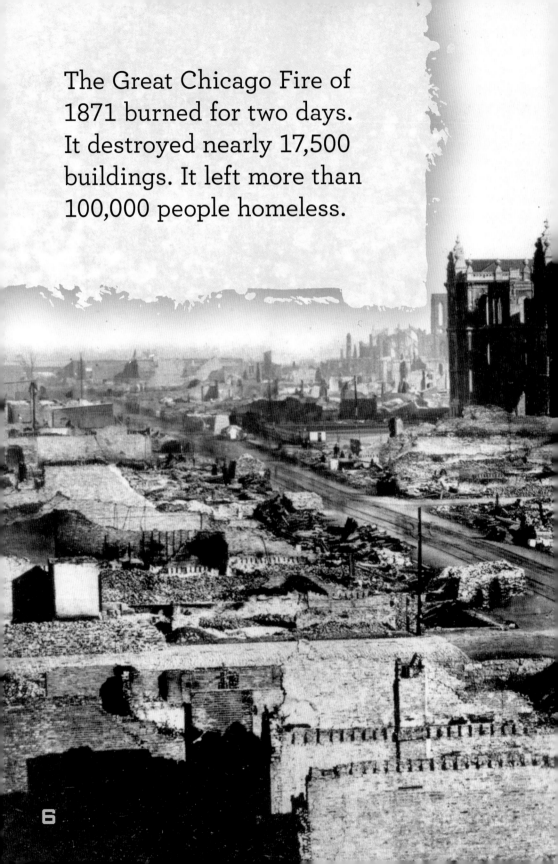

The Great Chicago Fire of 1871 burned for two days. It destroyed nearly 17,500 buildings. It left more than 100,000 people homeless.

7

PREPARE

Most **uncontrolled** fires can be avoided if people take the right steps. Check your home for **flammable** objects, like clothing, paper, and **aerosol** spray cans. You should keep all flammable things away from any type of heat.

Make sure all of your **smoke detectors** have batteries and are working properly. Having a **fire extinguisher** and knowing how to use it will also be helpful.

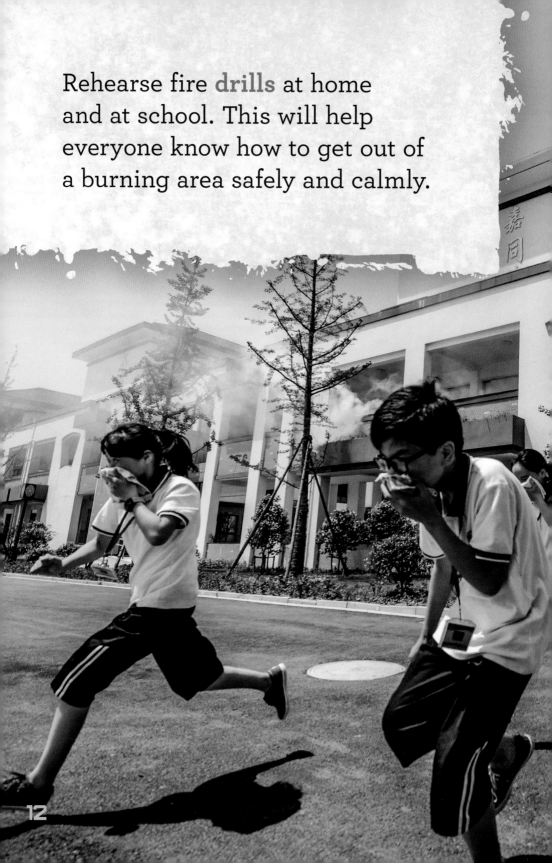

Rehearse fire **drills** at home and at school. This will help everyone know how to get out of a burning area safely and calmly.

SURVIVE

When you **evacuate**, bend down or crawl. Smoke rises and can hurt you faster than the fire will.

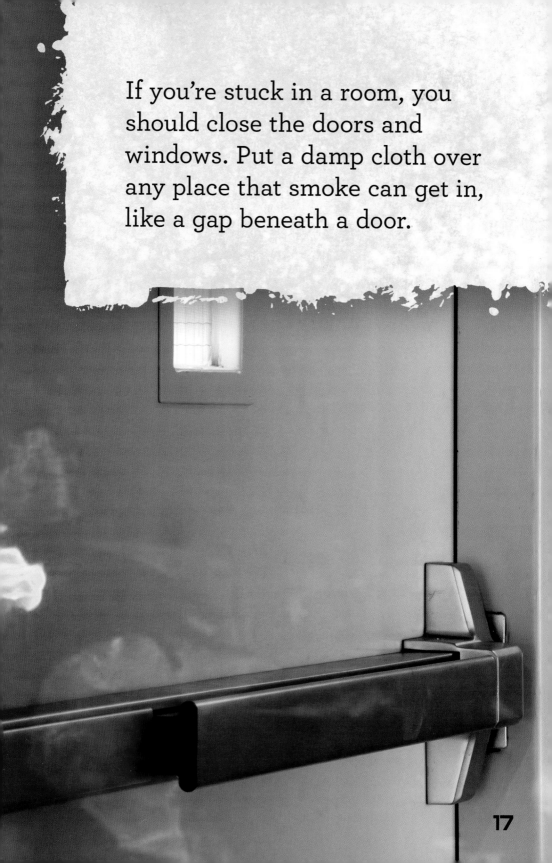

If you're stuck in a room, you should close the doors and windows. Put a damp cloth over any place that smoke can get in, like a gap beneath a door.

Feel for heat by touching closed doors. A warm door is a sign that there is fire on the other side. If it is warm, you should leave through another door or window.

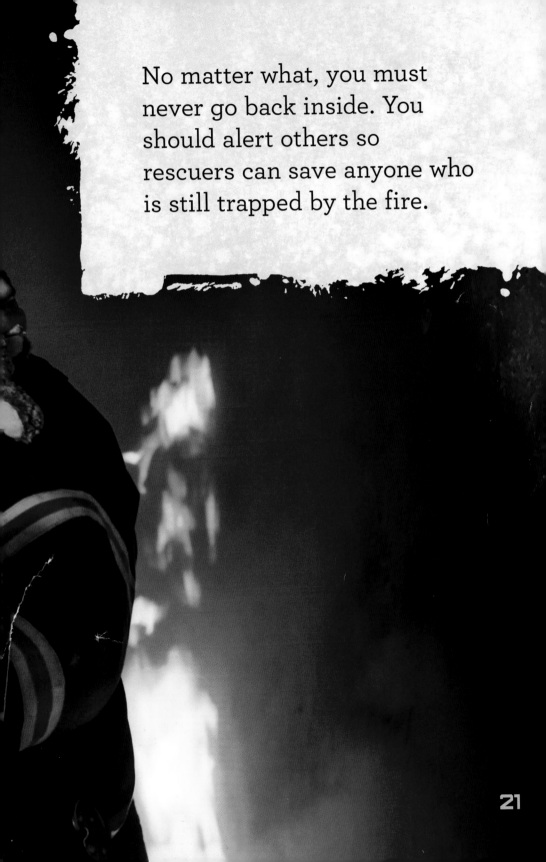

No matter what, you must never go back inside. You should alert others so rescuers can save anyone who is still trapped by the fire.

GLOSSARY

aerosol – a substance contained under pressure that is able to be sprayed.

drill – instruction and practice of a routine.

evacuate – the act of leaving or being removed from a place, especially for safety reasons.

fire extinguisher – a compact device that helps put out fires with water or foam.

flammable – easily set on fire.

smoke detector – a device that gives a warning of the presence of smoke.

uncontrolled – hard to stop or control.

ONLINE RESOURCES

Booklinks
NONFICTION NETWORK
FREE! ONLINE NONFICTION RESOURCES

To learn more about surviving a fire, please visit abdobooklinks.com. These links are routinely monitored and updated to provide the most current information available.

INDEX